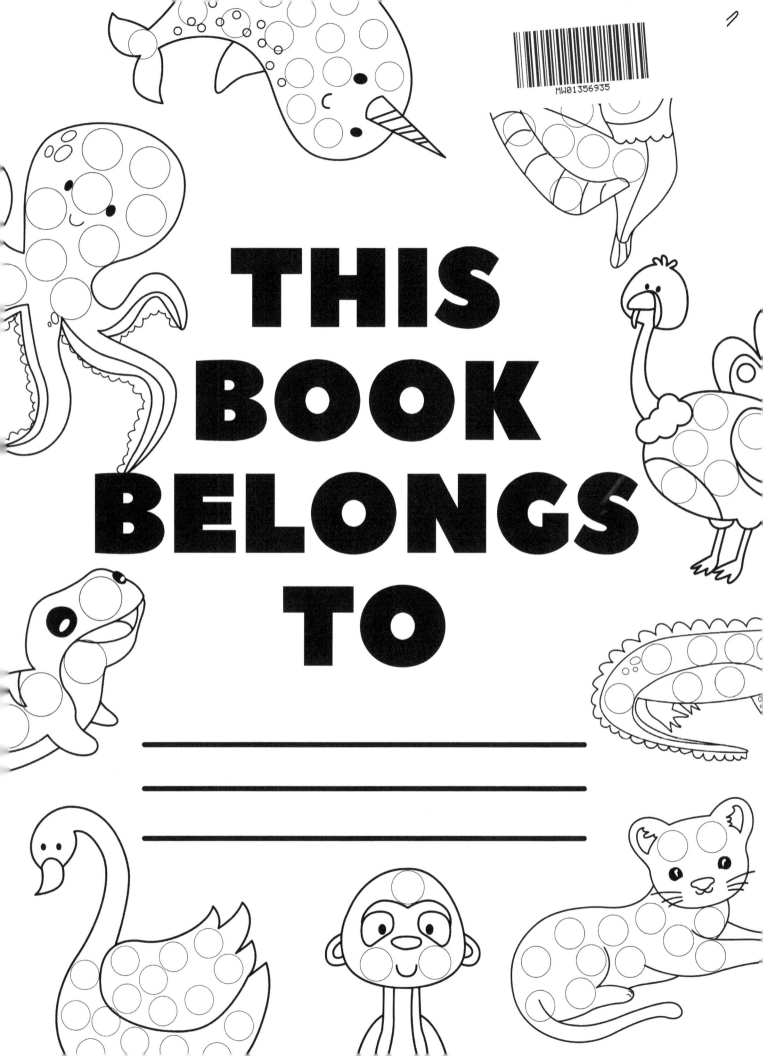

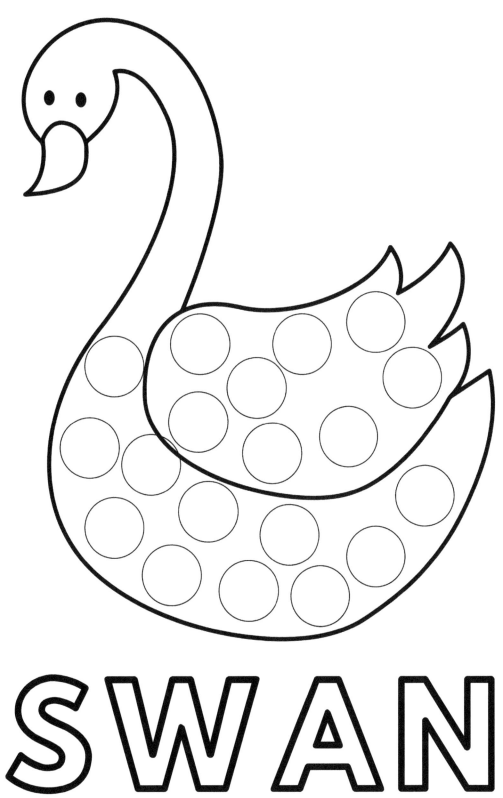

SPIDER

PIG

UNICORN

PANDA

PENGUIN

ZEBRA

PEACOCK

RACCOON

MEERKAT

LIZARD

RABBIT

OCTOPUS

WOLF

MONKEY

CAT

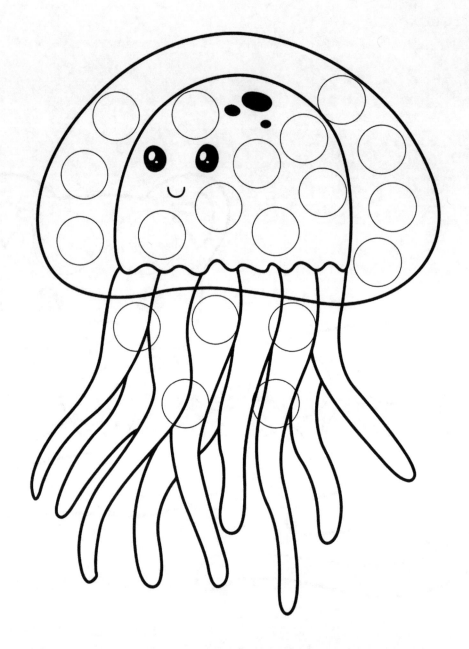

JELLYFISH

BIRD

LOBSTER

CARACAL

SNAKE

HAMSTER

GOAT

BEE

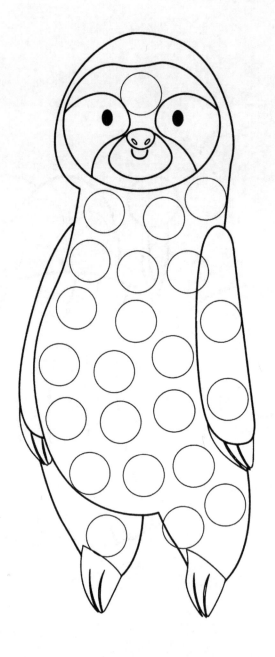

SLOTH

BEAR

HORSE

CROCODILE

HEDGEHOG

ELEPHANT

REINDEER

HIPPO

LADYBUG

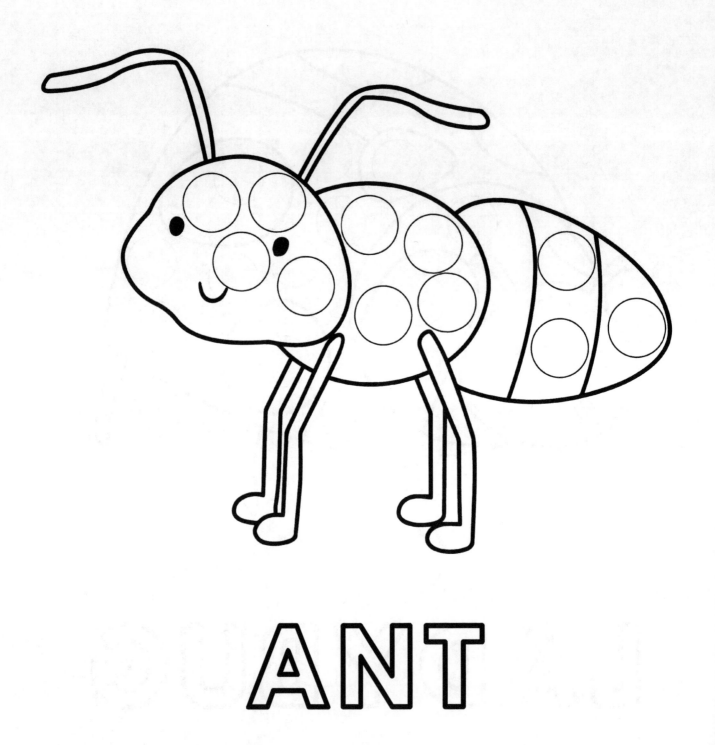

RAT

DOLPHIN

DRAGONFLY

DRAGON

FISH

FLAMINGO

CAMEL

KANGAROO

FROG

T-REX

BUFFALO

PIGEON

PIGEON